Rebar Moss

New and Selected Poetry

Tom Quirke

Copyright © 2020 Tom Quirke

ISBN: 9798694434232

PublishNation
www.publishnation.co.uk

Contents

Lysander's Cage

You come to me when the sands are dry
When redemptions silk foot is no longer near
And the evening sunlight is gasping.

You fell between sharp turned edges
Found comfort in the different
And forsaken -
But all the while your scented
Breath clung to my air.
A chalice of you,
Stung on the living memory
Hewn onto my shadow and footsteps
Yet taken.

The porous earth that connects us always
Tides laced with your whispers
And the crush of your daydreams;
Draws hot rain from the mountains
To fall on my mind eternal.

Etain's Lure

I made a spine of branches
Twine woven and flung into
The forest lake.
For a time, the warm evening
Held the surface together
And the hook lay in the wave.
Slipping down eventually
Weariness cupped me and
My eyes slipped down with it.

I awoke between two moons
One nailed to a pitch sky
A piercing torch
Through the fabric of night,
Backstage light pouring through.

The second shook near my feet
Green lacquered ripples grasping
Silver reflections
Clashing over and under
Clamouring for sacred space.

At the heart of the battle
My sunken line, a foreign harpoon
Plunging enemies together,
Behind the stick was bending
Curtsying to an unseen weight.
Then the rod began to shake
            - Divination found.

Marauding up from black depths
Came a bubble thickened bellow,
An eruption in the night that snapped the
Woodland creatures into silent hiding.

As glass un-shattered
The lake top sealed.
Freezing mist like rolling fingers
Clawed through the evening air
Scratching their way
Skyward, blowing a
Silvery cloak around the water's edge.
On high branches dipping leaves
Parted warm drafts above
Ice shackles under.

A rising scream shattered the
Shimmering cage and
A goddess was flung into the air -
Roaring at the new world
Straining for the starlight.

As lungs and blood contorted,
Newly born in the air,
Scales of magenta and ruby fell
Unhooked in the splash
Pelting the lake with jewels
That gulping fish succoured and
Quickly took down.

Landing on edge lapped stone
A storming mist blew around
Mud in touch of her skin became marble
And the bedrock
Concaved a throne.

The glacial whisper withdrew.
Mirrored crystals acquiesced, releasing
Themselves back
In peace to their brethren and
The lake lay tide-less
Unstrung from the thaw.

I heard animal breath on the fog.
Deep panting ploughing over silence.
Every sunken footprint closer
Greater temptation was revealed -
Red hair glowing like burnished gold
Curled in heat and falling around her
Though a shawl of breeze kindled embers.

Her spring white skin
Almost dry with newness
Prickled in the air -
Wore the moons light
As a veil.
Stained only by a crimson line
Running from a tear washed fissure
On a flawless cheek.

Hooked now, I drew closer
Creeping beyond the dewy curls
As one emerald eye, faceted
With fire touched hazel,
Looked into my bones knowing it
Had me snared.

A slender arm rose from her side
Palms wiping the blood
And the corner of her pink
Lips rose like birdsong.

The emerald eye,
All the time lacing my soul with fine braids
Flickered once down on bare ankles
Bound now in cheap twine and hook.
I knelt
Lifting her feet to my lap, she was
Unbound
My fingers pushing along warm
Beeswax skin
The soft scar gently rubbed away.

Daring to look up from my labour
Her voice came to me, full as a choir.

"What is your lover's name?"

Afraid to say I whispered only that I had none.
Her touch came again as
She placed in my hand a pebble,
An orb of cold parting our
Fingertips.

"Think of your lover and cast the stone.
For every foot the pebble falls I will give you
A decade.
For every skip the pebble makes
A child."

The stone held tightly
I saw the good years before me
My arm flung back, to loose
Old dreams across the water.
But spinning past I stretched
Beyond and kissed her
Rage and love filled her eyes
She wrapped her arms around my neck
And took me to the deep.

On every chance
Naked in the summer
Crooked in the winter
I swim.
Long threads and hooks from my toes
Rake the lakebed.
Lures from my fingers
Dance between the water and the air
Always she slips
My snares
She will not
Bite.

Currach

part one

Forrest bones, re-blooded in tar
Dried in-shore wind lay
Slanted on morning stones,
Skinned in the foreign hides
Of grass sifters.
Slides now
From soil to sea.

Changing tides lap the side of the currach.
An applause caressing unfamiliar skin
Gently drawing on to deeper waters
As a half-heard song in the distance.
The kelp kingdom thins underneath
And the surface below drops away,
Their ebbing fingertips no longer able
To touch two worlds.

Further out the brine cackles
Of gulls rejoicing at land
Become distant and silence,
But for the waves,
Gradually consumes.
The currach idles over the surface
A patient seed, swept
From the earth and the
Traction of life.

The oars ease round their crook
Each lift, waiting for the fall.
Waxed and rounded timber
Sinks into the waters tip

Smoothly, binding the barrier.
A wooden splinter between
Two kingdoms. A connection felt
In places fingertips cannot
Learn to callous.

Peering from the currach edge
Sand has given back to pebble waiting
Boulder to sunken rocks.
In dark stasis they lay
Too far from the winds touch
Moons whispers
Too Far from the sunlight.
They breathe decades and
Centuries. Molluscs moving as
Stone bees over an
Ancient slow hive.

Oars clip the backs of waves and
The currach glides
Further from the last ground.
Its shadow now stretched
In the deep water
With nothing more to fall on.

It rests now.
A point on the horizon
Encapsulated between
The endless sky vault
And sea-cellar.
A shell of life
Squandering between
Vastness.

Cloud Plough

Nestled on hill's chest
Another June morning
Cirrus lay to the east, thinking
As it does.
I cast up my fishing line
Golden hooked and tipped with
New memories,
To lace their soft edge and
With the ease of milk over silver
I drew the thin flock
Across the sky.
It parted to the West
Swifter now with the
Thoughts I had shared.

I awoke in the afternoon
The nimble altostratus shadow
Over me though a blanket.
Rolling grey, frayed with
Ocean white tips
Hung as painters' oil
Frozen in the sky,
Abundant with prospects.
But I was seventeen and
Impatient for fate to
Fall from its edges.
I flung a harpoon of swift wood
Piercing its middle.
In fierce silence
Sunlight began to gnaw
At new chasm edges and
When the sky cleared the

Birds in the trees began to talk
Of unexpected fruits.

I could not rest through the evening.
From a great distance
I had heard in my heart's chambers
Craters of agitation broiling,
Glazing the heavens with torment
And sucking the light in
Evenly from the North.
Then, slowly at once
Nimbus swallowed the sky whole
And came to me like a mountain
Gorging on warm air
Strobed with flashes of
Malice and doubt.

Snatching green vines
I tethered myself to the hillside
And shot a great anchor
Of clay into its turbulent soul.
The beast curdled
And as hot rain bled down
I roared back at the thunder.
My feet sunken in the land,
Over hours I fought and
Twisted my bones to
Wrench the torment South
To a future horizon.

When enough time had passed
Fires of fog cleared to evening light.
My soul was scarred
And I had aged.

Under a clear sky, panting
I waited for the moon
And her understanding.

September Crush

Scraping hoof on concrete, clattering
Reverberates on the walls of the pen.
Impatient sticks slash through air as
Mud flecks scatter across stagnant floor
Never to colonise.

The sloping toe slides on its mud hoof
Sharpening when the stab of the hard floor
Shudders up the beast's flank,
As for the first time the ground
Fights its weight.

Roaring as hooked nose
Cleaved by brass
Is dragged into the air,
Balloon black eyes search the ground for resistance
But the thick neck straining -
Has too rise.
And amongst the
Swish of tail and calloused slap,
Back legs grind forward.

Troughs of newly laid muscle and flesh, bursting
From thickening bone
Hanging firmly on the frame -
Are navigated through the miserly gate.
Red rusted iron pinioned to dead rock
Wails as the weight of the animal is forced through.

The flush of hot breath
Stab of boots
And clamour of the morning's commotion,
Are drowned in the air
By the clatter of the closing gate
        - land locked away
And the silence of capture.

The hose comes on, cold and fierce.
Stolen lavender scents raze the mud
As field tattoos are washed to the gutter.
The summers tan and dirt, excoriated
By high pressure civility.

Clippers buzz as hands and scissors
Shave and shorn the baulking skull.
Blonde locks sliced to the floor
Though antlers unused
To unrecognised reflections.

Loose toes crammed into black shoes,
No longer to splay in the grass
Or feel the dew,
The lace draws the bones tightly.
Drawing in the next sprint
To a crawl.

Last, worst, the cotton chain
Green and yellow woven noose
Throat locked and
Soul yoked.
The forward gate released
The tall ones still in their
Dirt rejoice;
'*There. You're all-ready now sweetheart.*'

Echo Line Station

Over the fall
Cresting the hour hand
Runs the endless river.
Corkscrew of time
Turning into the dial.
Forever the foreground until
Piercing and relevant
In a rupturing instant...

Between the tick of two clocks
Thoughts fall asunder.
Retinues on parchment screens
Ever-wave of candelabra pixels
Stop broadcasting.
A lost roman numeral, rolling rogue
Over station tower face.

The delicate glide of pleasantries and gratitude's
Slumps now in windless corner, smoking under roof.
Billowing bit lip and fog of clenched tut
The trickling wildfire of inconsideration
Fanned wider by its loathers.
Smearing clean air with discontent
And exhausted malice.

Above rests kaleidoscopic intent
To meet and greet and holler and chat -
Evaporated now between two breaths.
Not to cancel, not to be late
But never to go at all.
Seeing now the dirt shackles
Grime incumbent of duty promised
Darkening glass eaves
With the grot of time wasted.

Wandering pigeon iridescence, gleams
Like mountain dew over distant teal canopy.
Hobble and cock eye, lilts towards
Skylight and majesty of turquoise zenith.
Soot brushed air freckled with rain
Scythes through a palace without ironworks
A kingdom of vacant thrones.

Leather and cotton, cleaved in
Tempered mirror, soured in seasonal tones
Speckled now with tamed halogen lighthouses
Strands you naked, unrecognisable
In a shroud of your own breath
Buried in what was your shadow.

Whitewashed ambition sheds like
Returning pebbles, sharpened
Then dulled on same tide.
Bricks from fallen bridges are found
Byroads cleared and
Oil lamps glow again in forgotten houses.
Old music begins to warm, until
Leaves rise to the tree
A bell rings backwards
And you hear familiarity
Garbled on a tannoy - as
Every voice tells you
'If you don't go now
You will never make it.'

...before boring a deep mine
Seams of memories
And an echo loud enough
To guide the chiselling hand.

Blasphemy

When they built that house they planted trees all round it.
Sprawling shoots wrenched, then
Fallen into a shovel's neat hole.
Creating a boundary of nature, to nature.
Thorns marched and saplings hardened.
But the bracken was maligned, verges held venom.
On the hilltop inclines, woodland roots soured
Nascent tendrils quenched in the damp.
Soon after, fangs in the wind shredded the bark
Innards cracked out to rain, rivulets washed the sap
Dredging amber blood back to the soil.

The man from the county office, wouldn't stand on grass
Said they would have to come down, scuppered and felled.
So, saw chewed on timber forsaken since seed
And strangled lumber was slain then sliced.
The blistering range choked on them briefly;
Gluts of weak smoke spat out to the hillside
Perfuming the house with cannibal cologne.

But the dwelling was exposed now. The hills breath whistled
On this single tooth, revelled on lone target
Whipped its endless vapours into barbs and lashed
The walls with nails of rain, claws of frost.
Splinters of water endlessly sought weakness to kiss
Hidden trenches to amass, recesses to bulge
And bones to bend on.

When drenching finished rest-bite brought
Seeping heat, proud paint dimmed as chemicals cured.
Unionised flecks, backstabbed by fractured wrinkles
Were shorn to the ground in exhaustion.
Rusting hooks let slip tiles, cracked then
Shattered by their midday chores.

17

There was a point, a time of rescue
Where the banks sheaf could have halted the surrender
But the look of the place sunk any appetite.
Wrangled weeds, like soil bred barnacles, soon found succour.
Their trellis reach clambered higher with months, tarmac pocked
Walls breached - not long after the car was gone forever.
With no furnace to repel the cold, the retreat to wild
Was swift. A swathe of green came to swallow the partitions
A bandage to capture the rot.
One winters day after school they told me the roof had broken
Spine snapped under snowfall,
Bricks scattered to the floor
Ambitions abandoned.

In one of the summers after, there was a fire set loose.
It claimed the slow turning wood, scoured the plaster and paint.
The rubble was scavenged that autumn.
Dropped into a pond concerning some farmer.
Foundations were weed woven, cracked and given over
As the field ate across its wound, grass growing over the debris
Soil swallowed and washed down.

We still talk of that house sometimes, the older ones
Chawing roll ups on the byroads, to convince ourselves
It had been there at all.

Shorelines

On broken shore
Stray lapwing bound in failed retreat
Spies from cloying sand
Electric whips, ever brighter,
Purged plasma thrashing
On distant clouds.

Loose cracked sand
Fills fat barnacles
Along the sea edge.
Unchained waves ride
Into evensong fissures.
Upbraided kelp flounders on
Drunken rocks and
Swollen gull's beak gasping whelks
From their briny tomb.

Cry and caw fill lashed air
While underneath frittering antennae
Duel against incumbent sands
Fearful of golden arcs.
Kingdom mounds are flicked up
Translucent shells,
As they await the moon in
Quaking portcullis.

Northerly ditched grass seed
Flung by wind onto dunes,
Flounders in albino soils.
Un-purposed to suck the salt sea
Nor tangle in the frayed undergrowth
Already tangled in itself
Their corpses are freed on the wind.

Waves scarify with torn blue fingers
Nails of froth clawing the earth
In raking hate and bitter duty.
The beach twice sanctified in cold embrace.
A singular ladled drop, overexerted
Released from the ocean
Onto porous shore, rewarded for its
Infinite motion by unconditional inertia, as
Eastwards the sun and its bloom
Are devoured.

Blasted heat roared from
Tight coals in tight rows
Snatched out into the night with
Burning stupor and vivid embers.
Quick flurry against a coal pit sky
Expecting return to compressed pitch,
The hot breath exhausts in fright
Halves in fear
At the shore.

From the town singing,
Between tides churn,
Church bell rung by summoned wind.
Tune caught on seaward breeze
Strays out among savaged decks
Spreading its call as a forgotten whisper.
At shores lap, old sailors stare in
Towards village lights
Salt tears rolling over
Their faces.

Coach to Holyhead
For Mum

The summer night was new to me.
I had grown used to long outdoor games,
Cordial from the fridge and sleeping on top of sheets
Until salmon fog of sunset fell like the last blanket
To never quite darkness.
But school finished today and as soon as we got home
She told us she had spent the day packing and
For six weeks, we were going 'home'.

We would have to stay up late, the coach didn't leave until ten.
Unrecognised television programmes rolled over the screen.
Actors giddy with emotion; shouting, kissing, crying and fighting
As we were perched, nervous in waiting.
Finally, the time came to leave and we leapt gladly into twilight.
The evening air blew over me discovering a new geography
Another side of everything I had known to be all.
Streets were quiet, but this was not slumberous winter dark
Looking to roll deeper in cotton and downs,
This was a darkness of nascent movements
A stirring that could not be seen
But anticipated, tantalised on fine hairs.
We moved then quietly with purpose
Like cubs between dens.

Thin marigold lights jutted from coach flank
A strange hemming of trapped energy and warning.
The engine idled noisily as though it too was restless
For the burden of stillness to be uncoupled.
Old suitcases were carefully loaded into the underbelly
As though the beast fed on our folded hopes and preparations.
The driver stretched and patrolled
Talked narrowly in smiles and paced the length,
Eager for the waiting to become the doing
But fearing its demands all the same.

I hurled myself into a window seat, only thinking
To check with her after, but she was happy.
Excited acknowledgements buzzing
Coats removed and placed above.
As I played with levers to the side
Nets on the seat ahead, unnoticed
A quiet calm strengthened.
People around the edges slowly faded.
Parked cars slunk away then last cigarette was flung;
The wayfarer's torch abandoned on foreign kerb.
When the coach door closed, fat rubber suckering around the seals
There was discernible relief – they couldn't take it from us now.
An aluminium partition from the city
Had sliced us, from them.
From the rigid school and endless shop
Church calendar, abandoned bus stop.
The neighbours, clubs, people and pets.
Time stealers. Dream feeders.
Rule makers. Money takers.
And those drenched in the weight
Of having nowhere else to go –
       We were separated now
And as the wheels began to roll
Anchors strained and snapped.
Binding ties were sheared
And with one rotation
Obligations cleaved.

Streets became roads and houses ran together in my vision.
In minutes, everything I recognised as my range
Was behind me. Every bend in the road
Motorway sign, bridgehead and slip road was newness
Washed in pale motorway lights and guttural speed.
Outside now, the glow of the coach, ricocheted through the gloom
As a firefly deserting the colony.
Beyond my window the house, street and traffic lights
Had been enveloped by the thickening darkness.
I winced my eyes to see habitat amongst the black
But as we travelled further the lights were harder to find.
More and more I was staring only at my detached amber ghost
Drifting untethered aside my window.

We climbed and the gargle lifted to a roar
As pistons grew red in determination -
Not to be slowed or caught.
Sweeping left, far away and dropping down
A valley of lights was revealed. A last
Orange and white constellation, fallen and fixed
Staunched into position by colossal soot sky.
The embers not quite a patchwork,
Fiery hues distorting but failing to reach each other.
Burning alone instead
Like failing matches, slung
Surrounded and isolated
Awaiting the smother of midnight's cloak.
Each a home and a house and a warm bed
Getting further away
Then vanishing
From my eye
And then my mind.
I turned to my Mother, who did not speak but
Lowered my head onto her lap,
Stroking the hair behind my ear.
As I stared at the shadows,
Coming over in relentless waves,
She understood I had seen too much.

Wasp

The doors to your home are open.
Silence inside sequinned with sugar.
Forsaken lumps of jam on delft radiate
Carmine allure.
Easing against soft current
I enter freely,
Owning my direction.

Your domain is clamped in stillness.
As I devour
Bounty of your waste
I think on different kingdoms
I have lingered.
Yours is rigid, untouched by air's tides.
Moored unequivocally to deep earth
Fixed beyond erosion.

Wrenched flower stifled on sill.
Water fettered in sand-blown prison.
Lights breath filtered and thinned.
Storm diluted,
Rain does not touch here,
Does not weave loose seed through
Grounds, rise green leaf replenished
To the sky.

Your home is death to me.
Now I understand.
You have bred the motion of life
From it
Replaced it with frictionless teeth
And quenched ashes.

25

My greed took me here
But before I am gorged
I am trapped within
A snare as lavish as it is
Absolute.

Until now, always a fissure
Fence crack, wall hoop
Rock pile snag
Leaf on a river
But this inertia cage
Matches my hatred with perfection.
Leeches my frustration
In binding fatigue.

I await morning then,
Watch the sun falling
Exhausted from its mantle
Sting from its heat, spent.
I cannot feel its warmth here
There is no taste in the air or
Breeze splitting between my wings.

I may die tonight
Staring out at what once
Was all mine.
I can see gentle evening yawn
Waving among tree boughs.
Can see clouds fumble over firmament
Loading heavens with tomorrows streams
Glistening flowers lolling as they close.

I know the dew is coming
But I cannot feel its ripples,
I cannot taste the ebbs.
In slender solitude the moon rises
My regrets fall like shadows on the fields
I pray for daybreak, a forgetful gaoler,
More life
And freedoms to choose from once again.

Hill Stone

Stood, rotten footed
Between yellow tipped
Furze and shimmering muck
I snide autumnal mulch;
My claw boot windlassing,
Thumping trench
Upending nettle tomb
Briar's catacomb
Thistle crypt and
Failed seed husks. The
Snagging rock
Whacked from clenched soil
Spills on the surface,
Energy erupted.
Its edges tumble in
The unbound
Freedom all over
Pirouetting atop expanse.
Earth unlocked
Sky plunge
Quick then slow
Until motion ceased.
The first stillness selects
Compass points
New face to heaven
Seeking penitent rain.
Fortress borders adapt
To foreign fields
Whilst conquered shore is bedded
Waxed in clay
And cathartic slumber.

Two foot travelled
In thirty years.
With hurling stick, I could
Swiftly slash the stone
Furlongs from its bedrock.
Could kick it down the road
Or take it home, dangled
In a torn pocket.
But what am I
To interrupt, perhaps
The footfall
Of a hare darting
From red fur teeth?
Perch of a robin
Foretelling worm's abdication.
Laming jewel in heifer's hoof
Meaning she cannot be sold?
Whetstone sparking under claw
Of the hill monk praying
From his sett.

Jammed between two worlds
Accustomed to neither
Wanted by none.
Awaiting deep burial
Under tractor wheel,
Fixed in the hill.
Fate's pinioned, as
Time under my eyes erodes
The stone waits as a
Gravestone un-carved
Hiding from the mason and
Mortal clock
Too fleeting to fathom
Pondering its touch.

The Lough

Slicing more time from skin's sheaf
My fingertips touch down to sink
Water, unexpectedly
Cool like the lough in June -
Summers heat slow to touch its depth.
On the shore, where ripples tantalised
Bare feet offered us naive trust.
Our calves and knees were easily tricked
But by the time we were waist deep
We had displaced the equilibrium
And the pure cold of fresh water
Punctured the transitory balmy surface.
Soles bending to bedrock
Toes sinking for silt
We stood, naked in new bodies.
One half burning in snow melt
Cleansed and rejuvenated
One half a sail for the evening sun
Turning for the last warm billows.
But we had a decision to make and
As our simultaneous chatter calmed
I caught the lakes reflection
Flickering within your pupil-
Alive in your soul already.
Reaching out
Freshly anointed fingertips
Chilled and glistening, clasped
As eyes lit and lungs drew down
We dove.

Just now, I felt your face tremble on water top
The beam of your voice topping small ripples.

Midnight's Fox

Curled, coat turned to draft
Rumpen bristles spun towards a threshold
Sensing the day on fine tips.
Dew lifting, heat tricking through the ground.
In the come and go of sullen winds
Days are measured in events
Unheard from thickened snug
Barrelled in hair.
Instead divined
As tremulous cows vibrant the land
Daylight falls between farm buildings
Frost as silvered poison
Seizes the grass
And glistening moonlight
Splays as breath unending.

Rising out from the warm,
Where dampness kindled in riddled fur,
A leathered snout draws down
Thimbles of evening air.
Enticement dappled and ice polished
Laced with carcass and egg
Hidden in solitude, kept by wilderness.
These lighthouse scents
Drawn deep into scavengers' lungs.

As sinews straighten
And the crescents of slumber shaken
Two ears unfurl, pricking to fears
Of all that is not heard
Between tightened heartbeats
And its own pad drenched footfalls
Flickering between crunching leaves.

The field is stagnant with midnights grip.
Walls of stone patchwork darkened
Corrupted by the shadows of moon's carelessness
Enchanting all that would move
Emanating immobility and
Pulling tight the soil roots
Till the land is rigid.

But moving now,
Paws trickling over
Too quick to be snared by stillness
An auburn pelt trotting and scurrying
As though a rune of yesterday's blood
Rejecting sedation
Lifeful in the temporary cadaver
Hunting revival.

Fisherman's Bow

Coming onto daily darkness
His numb fingers slid the noose
From rigid iron mast.
Tension in the cord, lost
And tossed to stern
Curling as an eel, abated.

The boat rocked gently
As the Fisherman's weights
Were accepted by the sea.
Engine kindled stolen fire
As gauges in the wheelhouse
Registered tame sparks.

Felloe spun, drifting to lay lines of the cove
Turning the Fisherman from slanted village.
Oil chewed chunter hauling him
From the quay, ringing the brass bell
Three times he signalled to whitewashed homesteads
Every light to douse, sin over shame.

Cerise hull surged over the sea
As fingerprints of waves
Splayed and fell from its sides.
Oak scrubbed deck caught
All that was left of the sunlight
And a summoned gust swept clear the path ahead.

He checked between panorama rolls,
There was no rig or ship
No foreign illumination
Creaking alongside the night,
No beacon of spiralling spyglass
Land locked, grimacing at the motion.

Above the helm the Fisherman lit a candle
Lone ember, loves cadence
Shivering on abyss of worlds cliff.
Then around the boat switches flicked
Bulbs rekindled static flame
Tepid light waving back from black water.

When the engine stopped
The sound of oceans shadow bloomed.
Strong winds pealing on waves
Fraying sea skin, ringing the brass bell
Six times he watched the bow descend
As a sweet red leaf lost to a river.

Bubbles crushed over gunwale
Gorging on virginal space
Breeding in flurry.
Soon the deck washed with hungry tide
Varnish locked pond emerged, existed
And was swallowed by its brethren.

The surface devoured gently.
Water rose up wheelhouse glass
Rushed the roof, and dropped
Into lap of the aft deck
Securing its whole heaviness;
Dragging them down from above.

In the blue, silence
Escaping air fractured and gulped
Without popping, rooftop waves
Fumbled and acquiesced.
Calm engorged the ocean's belly
Carrying down as a seed through pulp.

As the glow of empires dwindled
The candle took hold, richer
And brighter with every
Passing fathom, lumens
Feasting on the dark,
Candescent aria billowing in the bleak.

At sand kiss the crimson boat
Levelled and a thousand years of bones
Raced briefly for moonlit crown -
Snatched release
And fell again as a fog
Of ancient journeys.

The curled rope, free of its iron bite
Spun and flickered and loosed
Twisted to life by outlying cadaverous scents
Slid away from the lanterns.
Their brass shine trickling over
New scales.

The Fisherman spread calloused fingers
Pushing into deep wave.
Feeling the thick of the water.
Brine mangled and stifled in pressure
Its stagnation matched
By its turmoil.

The kneaded rump of the fiddle
Nestled between jaw and shoulder.
Sawing the bow, over and back
Music seeped into the ocean
As ink spreads on pristine canvas
And starlights echo is bled.

Notes drawn from his fingertips
Danced over taut reels
Racing the melody,
Flinging themselves from wooden bridge
Leeching along trench and ravine,
Though yew roots creeping through centuries.

In lunar hollow;
Morass of the forsaken
Astride blind creatures and
Thin tentacles
Eking harvest from motes -
A shimmer grew.

Over and round the verses blew,
The Fisherman's fiddle lashing the water
Faster and harder.
A far sunken mist grew to a cloud
Fretted sliver on hurricane winds
Charging now in immaculate starvation.

The gloom beyond the candles reach
Began to speckle,
Flecks of distant reflection growing
And with it a thrashing zeal.
Altered chorus, gnawing feverishly
Chasing desire back to the Fisherman.

In a horde of gilled commotion
Funnels of lust and need
The fiddle drew its last note.
Erupting frenzy froze
In its own wake -
And the Fisherman knelt.

From the recess of the swarm
The Queen salmon slinked forth.
Examining the boat in
Gracious space newly abounded
Tracing bow to stern, for understanding –
Until the Fisherman stood.

Constantly cautious, her tail became still
Draught lulling her from verges,
Until her fin flexed
Holding her in place.
Just as streams of questions chased over her scales -
The Fisherman held out his hand.

Falling into magenta eye
He drew his hand through the water
Inwards to the boat.
When she hesitated he implored
When she did not sway
The Fisherman begged.

Tasting barley sweetened brooks
The flock, under divergent powers
Begun to thin towards
Estuary and inlet.
Unshackled from fealty
They swam quickly to fate.

Candle wax ebbing
The Fisherman's hand thrust out from starboard.
She curled into his soul
Turning in his fingertips as cool silk sliding
But swam away to emptiness
And all that could not be judged.

Lanterns dulled, famished on bitter cold
Florescence quaking, ringing the brass bell
Eight times he lay on the deck.
The boat rose as a wooden anchor
Released from wandering
Sped homewards.

Drowning in lonely air once more
An unfamiliar year began to soak against the horizon.
The Fisherman cast the remains of the candle
Far into the water, stared into the fingers
She had moved through and
Cried fresh tears back into the sea.

Honours

A peerless jewel of arched power
Wound in magnificence,
The kestrel clung in the air
Its marbled talons dug
To privy hook
As though it had chosen
To halt its majesty -
Allowing the worlds gaze
To fix on its splendour
Bloom in its opulence.
The servant zephyrs rolled around
Under and beside
Lifting King Falco to fine crystal airs,
Singular and applauded
Though unique nobility
Whose reign would not see landfall.
Lustrous speckles along outstretched wing
Vibrated between genuflecting breezes,
Sunlit stripes rippled
Pampered in the draft
As shimmering tail feathers arced
Waving gently.

When the moment came
Curling its wings downwards
Pivoting beyond all balance
It swept from the insular pedestal
Dashing to the grasses -
Its daily entitlement
Offset at once by quick death.
The serrated squeal of the rodent
Was all shock -
For it had seen the kestrel aloft
But had only applauded.

The Neb

On long starched sands,
Dimpled from the process of creation
Taut in perfection,
The edges of a land fixed.
Points pinioned
Tense in anticipation
And pristine reflection.
Until
A silver beak.
Shining peak on a invading shadow
Crosses the border.
Scratches though a honed spade on shingle
Lifts and falls as a razored needle
Weaving connections and separation.
Punctures as diamond edged drill -
Thirsting for blue geysers
And black volcanoes.
Then
Purity is wet with wounds.
Savaged in scored flecks
Slashes, crescent sweeps and
Languishing pools.
White soul tattooed
In wants, needs of the dammed;
Salvation of the thinkers
Kings blood
Paupers love.

Dry from battle, the island
Cuts adrift, folds to an envelope
Seeking harbour.

Submariner

(i)
I meet myself daily on gravelled slopes in time
As the weekdays long
Coming home I stand aside the shadow
Of my morning self, for fear we'd touch.

Urgently dredged from slumber
Soles slammed on thrashed rock rivers
A tempo of lateness beating a morning drum,
Stirs cats to their windowsills.
As numbed toes recoil though tender hoof
Cold legs shackled in habit find footsteps woven
By a semi-sleeping mind, awakened only briefly
Of moonshine cusping chimney stack
And buzzard cawing of her night's victories.
The orange clock marches guiltlessly forward
The pull of the hill throwing me down.
On the train, a captive shanghaied ten years ago
Slung into a carriage
A submarine on rails
Descending from freedom and the day.

(v)
As the doors split a vacuum is expelled.
Tired boots drop to concrete
Polish chipped, iron stairs steep
As waterfalls pen the platform.
But from the fathoms the stag rallies
Made desperate rejecting the fence
And leap, one step by two
Free of the dock to the foot of the hill.
As crewmates dispel to ginnels

The last leeching of my muscles
Begins with the hill climb.
Pride and exhaustion
Anger near defeat
Expense and loss,
All mix and stoke.
The fob watch by my lungs
Divining a new spring from the well
Hope released to muscle.
Shoelace shackles are stretched
Manacles torn.
With the punishment
Comes deep breath of
Air overflowing the plateaux
As sunrays calling on seabed.
Excoriating laden shoulders
Until camber evens, feet level
And all that is behind is below.

At home in ink
I practise cutting sandbags
From balloons
And imagine them drifting.

Vitruvian Boy

Arms wide.
Fingers spread.
Back turned
On all the world
That was known
As a sail
Cowled into pressing storm.
Hermits had fled
To cavernous shelter,
Huddled by hooks
Lamenting
Obligated will.
Cowards ran
Hiding among cobwebs
Taut as glass in silence.
Would be masters,
Fearful of conflict,
Beckoned angrily
From stifled tower.
But their rages
Were trounced
Fragmented
In torrent air
And we
Just laughed.

The last two
Abandoned
On a hail cleared battlefield.
Fates pinned
To tempest mast
An unspoken agreement
Of brothers in arms.
Commitments shredded to the fray.
Duties resigned.
Obligations deserted
The growing wind
Thrashing at our heels
I turned to check a smile
But the squall
Wrapped orange hood
His too
To just the glimmer of an eye,
Burning with life
Set free.

Shale under soles
Began to roll.
Last grip
Shedding loose.
Gale greased traction
Chiselling earthly weight
From its mooring.
When the first aqua alta
Of breath
From everywhere
That wasn't there
Struck,
We lifted free.
When second fell
Like thunder pouring
Our legs tripped forward
Descending hidden hill.
With the third,
Tidal bore
Calved from cloud mountains,
Thumped against
Our juvenile resistance -
We were flung
Shrieking loudly
Racing
Along the playground.

Harvest Rain

From the pillow, clamorous between other alarms
Canons of rain fasten the window
Sharpened droplets splinter on glass
Splitting to quick beads, fizzling on tile top.
I hear gutters gurgle, over-fat swells
Leaping from the sides, slamming summers table below
As if hoping to further flatten the iron.
The wind, a maestro thrashing timpani
And me
New-born to another October morning.
Thin melted sand, barricade all
Between my curled warmth and
Barrage of water stones outside.
A cruelty to sleeping ears,
As the lashes continue
And my head kneads between pillows,
I contemplate the night washing -
The pavement scuffs, reduced leaf
Misplaced muck, fingertips of trees
And cobwebs of dead spiders
Seared away by relentless transparent arrows,
Driven by an unseen passion.

Staggering between encased bulbs
Burning without heat
And forgotten decorations clinging to bush,
The din around my hood
And dripping fingers tell me I am now
Sequestered in the battlefield.
Evanescent purge fuelled in gales
Harrows on everything I possess.
My clothes darken

Painted in rain and new testament
Like a Monday baptism
On the souls of the forgetful
Rendered in wet ice
Landfall the only chorus.

With the new railway bridge
They had changed the direction of the water.
Dispersal was gathered
Then the collection raced together
And raged down grizzled fossil face.
Gentle wrinkles flushed in silver spearheads
Slashing from honed corner to crevice.
Bursting channels suffocated in torrent
Of gravity's tide swept by tempest whip;
Forced water to burst from the rock -
Ossified in anger
Purity tarnished
With all it had tasted.

Doors closed, I stood
Still pumiced by translucent shells
As freckled red lights, dimmed
And pulled away without me.
Growing in the pall
Behind the noise of sacrificed diesel
The rapture of the waterfall grew
Its ferocity gnawing on station pillars.

Alone, I crossed the tracks
And placed my hands in sharp cold
Fissure of ocean's pilgrims
Frantic in their mid-journey.
I let wash on my palms
Yesterday's footsteps
Now scoured from the village roads.
Dirt dried and chipped from my coat
Shoulder length blonde strands
Chocolate flecks
The breath as I had walked
Imbued with thoughts,
Harpooned to the floor and
Sluiced by fleeting invaders.
Washed in an unchartered surge.
Abducted by a nameless river.
Stolen to the sea.
Quarried to the deep.
A harvest of sullied water
Flavoured of our travails.
A feast
For that lurking dormant
Biding in the abyss.

The Fort

One February morning
We walked on the summit of the Downs.
Gales thrashed
Though leash gone rabid.
Blasting up the hillside
Clung tightly in punch full formation,
Before barrelling atop frenzied and free.
It wrapped my form as if polarised to heat
Relentlessly licking over vulcanised barriers
Until pouring on a tissue split.
Blowing off the dull cotton warmth
Until the frost fangs of it ate on my ribs
And the deep of my bones was cauterised.

Shallow footsteps began to slip
Traction blunted on shifting clay
As the wind sheared in half
Toppled by its own ferocity.
The swell shattered
Words between us, lost
Between mouth and ear
Snatched down ragged verges
To be listened too elsewhere.
Our breath fell into snares
Sluiced into valley shelters
As poached rain
Enriched in dewy comprehension.

With each sliding step
Wailed on and beaten
The trellis of us
Circled the fort.
Penitent heads bowed and staggered.
Perfumery and palm oils scoured
Dosed water diluted
Moistures excoriated.
It seemed we could not draw near
Until satisfactorily cleansed.
Admonished by the hillside
Like all who went before.

On the lip of the garrison
The pathway was lost.
Turned over and built up
Fallen and regrown
History almost hidden.
But the roots of the trees
Congregated there
Ran long and deep.
Thin sinews of ages
They sunk down to leech old barks
Their tendrils read over abandoned boughs
Suckled on ring laced loam
And wove through tawny synapses
Fusing with the bygone.

Standing in the circle's nave
You showed me where the fortifications
Once were stood.
Explained how the hillside defended
Clan after clan, legions and missions.
Set space for their ambitions to nurture
Grip and bud in fervour
Whilst ever eroding unbeknownst
Setting the land
Under time's plough.

Creaking by one then two
The green leaves present, swayed
Amongst evergreens listing
Incanting a toll;
That the wood carved for caskets
Trees planted over graves
Was soaked in the patron's wet ashes.
Whose offspring had built and burned
For the next generation
Thriving to decay
Their freedom pinioned on this pinnacle;
Binding them as timber ships in the soil
To journey through the same seas.

Black River

Falling in, tumbling down
Crushed by tussled blanket
Sown under the heat of coals,
Moulded islands of soft cotton
Form around you
A framework supporting your mass.
Exhaled cycles in the pillow nape
Torpor of used air rebounding
Like a tide between mountains.
Eye lids fall like thick sails
Over taut from offshore storms
Tired from the capes surrendered.

The black river begins to flow.
Rocks in the dam, melting.
Estuary sump recoiling out to the sea.

Adrift below
Kitchen words are unhooked
Sentences blur and different voices
Run together. Radio bells
Become meshed in drooping cadence
Until the beacon slips behind crescent moon
And the last note is crushed to a lull.

Tunnels of thought are sealed in
As mineshafts crumble, their
Boughs routed by twilight.
The signal from the lighthouse
Is finally broken.
Chains of light unbuckled.
The path ahead dissolves.
Resolutions are unshackled from promises.
Hopes run back into the pitcher
Corked carelessly with punctured hessian.

As limbs dismember
Muscles are flickered loose
Bones surrender their weight.
Foot soles depart
For nightly strolls
Up walls and
Over rooftops.

Blemished embers
Raise their hands for fixing.
Image blizzards and instructions
Roll calls of rules
Time keeping scores and
Manacles of propriety
Abated.
Queued.
Lodged in the blackout.
Misspelt and repainted.
Bunkered in the museum
Of the minds mosaic.
A new collection of inky tattoos
Chiselled and set
The colour bleeding between
Osmotic connections
Self-seeding
Forging intangible art.

Deeper, in obsidian trenches
Where inertia puddles
And doldrums list against each other
Thickening blood trickles to waning thump
A balance of entropy equates
Movement is just a memory
Words spoken are swept from porous ledger
In that near death
Disentangled and surrendered
Clockfaces' are fused
Past and future take company
Align and pass comment
On each other's choices.

Roaming the splendour, always
Citadel walls begin to drum.
Swelling arcs of thunder
Gnaw on fading barricade.
Cannonballs jagged with sirens
Clamour on ramparts.
Slack chains are summoned
Senses called back
Extremities reordered
And focused
Precisely.

Eyes struggle to open
Weary from travelling.
A stream of dawn air
Chilled from the dew
Sets new fires in the blood.
The machinery of this world
Has started up again
Ready for another shift.

The Bog Road

i

In the azure Cortina, I only sat in as a child,
I went driving between things I know
And the things I dream of.

Liquoring fuel on stranded promises
I inch the window down to an August evening.
Speed cooled air drawn in, emulsifies
In cabin heat as rendered wisps
Calved from eddies of perception
Tumble in fragments of radio.
Stray lyrics and forgotten harmonies
Pulse in the gaps of the engine
Note.

ii

Growing cracks on velveteen
Rubber licked road
Fleetingly saturated in tyre and
Absorbed through spring, send momentary
Tremors through the chassis.
Steel and bone frames soaking the bounce.

Red gauge held over *50*
Time and speed equalled.
White stripes strain
Thinning like months into years
As the countryside
Curls under my pressing toe.
The sound of existence outside

Suffocated by combustion as
Townships, old and new, merge.

iii

In stillness and synchrony
Amber and green glass
Flash to an empty road beyond
Disappearing after.
The squareness of the car swings
Heavily from the bend, slotting
Neatly on bush flanked lane.
The pull of the hill, slows.
Radio off, just the view
Ambling tyres and the applause
Of overreaching saplings.
As the worn fabric of the window lever
Turns in my hand so turns in the cogs
And barriers recede.

Engine crawling, numbed
Field sounds wane into the car;
The lowing of unseen cattle
Birds crashing hedges
Antlers clashing and
Loose gravel resisting the press back
Into weather broken tarmac.
A growing green weave emerges
A trench of grass splitting
The road, now
Stroking the foreign underbelly
Through fingers too supple
To grasp.

iv

I drive quietly past the sunset fire lighting
Of houses no longer standing,
But catch some kindness and forewarning in
Smoke signals from the
Thawing hearth.

Rolling the steering wheel starboard
The incline swells and
Potholes thicken.
Shadows of memory
Become fissures, absences cultivate
To ignorance and the blue bonnet sinks
Deeper each year
Like the heaving bow of a wayward ship.

v

Leaden now, the car scrambles quietly
Up the hillside
Fat with spent miles but
Dexterous as a beetle through the bog,
Twisting from the water's edge
Ever lured by the scent
Of ancient fodder.

Cresting the hilltop, the engine lurches
Onto the mesa and
Ebbing horizon plunges
To meet me once again.
Briars begin to flicker in the window
As a growing feast of thorns scrape paint.
Hedgerows thicken and shake with
Unseen vaulting creatures.
Famished road, narrows

Tar thins to mislaid stone
Until it is forsaken utterly
By its own reach.

vi

Ahead, an abandoned house I played in.
Turning the key towards myself
The unfelt tremble stops
To near silence but for the pangs
Of scorched metal
Doused in Westerly zephyrs.

The wild path, flanked with rushes and furze
Is just visible in the aching light.
Black water pools go undisturbed.
I kick down nettles and scoop under
Fallen beams, until I stand inside the gable end.
My outstretched hand traces
Movements from the past
Where my barbed penknife had bled the rock
When new dust falls from the seams
Of my scored initials.
Mountain squall gushes
Through hollow windows
Holding my face,
Breathing into my lungs
And I understand that I
Am bound forever.
That I had never left.

Slate
For Dad

Parked.
Engine rumbled to stillness.
We had found landfall in a lay-bye
Our churned bodies adjusting to sudden calm.
A spring draft writhing up from valley aside
Crept through the machine
Swabbing heat from scorched metal.
Pings and crackles rang from the chassis
A symphony of sweet moans
As the road sifting whale came to rest.

I opened the door, spun and
Dangled a pale thin leg from dusty seat.
Fresh air swarmed into the cab
Lifting cobwebs of new soot
Adding dew to the grime and
Liberating concrete dust to grease traps once more.

Coffee he asked?
I shook my head and slugged instead
From cordial, weak from heat.
As his hands worked the flask
My eyes idled over gorse
Stiffened to the ground
Only the very tips of which dared to tremble.
Looking above the brow of the wheel
Sipping coffee, fortified by home waters
I could not see what he saw
Or share his peace.

Reaching behind me, my tender fingers stretched
Past streaks of grain
Until finger and thumb just met
Around the handle. Saying nothing I
Swung the sledgehammer out
And jumped to the floor.
A rehearsed gymnastic vault
Performed in jeans ripped to shorts
And steel toe cap boots.

Idly patrolling the aft quarters
I checked the double tyres for masonry
Lodged between the two, perhaps
Halting our progress with
Unexpected synchronicity. But
Knowing truly any would have been shed already
Cast away on distant tarmac.
I turned the ash in my palm
Feeling the bias of the blunt head
Loading and slackening
The leaden potential, turning over and around
Circling itself.
Disliking the ponderous wait
Backfilled with unwanted notions and perplexities,
It pined instead for reflex and ferocity
And the clear headedness of instinct.

I meandered, hoping to oblige
Circumnavigating the wagon
In listless duty. Eventually
I crossed the empty road
And elevated on a ridge
Found an obelisk of slate.
Its elemental blackness
Striated out to greys and purples
Though it had been saturated by the heather

That now flourished all around it.
The crown of the block
Was flat and smooth
Had settled a millennium ago
And gone unchallenged ever since.

Beginning my calculations
I first tried to push it with my boot
But the mountain's tooth stayed firm
Thickly wedged in the jaw.
I stalked back and forth
Cooley surveying, then placed
Both feet on top and stomped,
My presence absorbed and
Met with indifference.

HIT IT! He said.
The coffee was gone.
With arms folded now over open window
He stared down at me from the gallery
Laughing.
I drew up the handle from flattened bracken.
With my right hand clenching the base
My left three quarters up -
Primed to channel all my might,
I swung the hammer heft
Behind then aloft. Freely
The staunch head plunged
And smashed its dead weight onto
Unmoving monolith.
Where not a speck of magma stirred.

Again. He said.
My eyes flit at his
Then back to the work, quickly.
Removing an oil infused jumper

I looked back, sure of my error.
The second swing was sweeter than the first.
Bending my knees I dragged the steel brick
Descending through the sky. Cracking sweetly
It shot a dull thud deep into the volcanic core
Tempting an eruption -
But nothing more.
The metamorphic altar remained impervious
Save flecks of white dust, scorches
Shorn from the equilibrium of conflict.

Not immediately, but I looked back
At the earnest face, labour tanned skin
And eyes, blood-shot with miles.

     Just once more. He said quietly.
Calluses were budding
Like fat stings on my tame hands.
Treacherous splinters knifed fingers
As unfamiliar pains cascaded
Beyond the muscle.
The sweat on my brow
Had begun to flow and stick.
Lungs panting, seeking urgently
A second born breath.

I glared down at the enduring rock
A boulder in my riverbed
And fixed on the perigee of stifling lava.
As the pared wood swooped
Round and down
It split the air
And loosed onto it
An anvil of callow rage
Powered in surety
And a bitterness of purpose.

Fracturing the central cloisters
Inertia shattered and with clamouring resolve
     - The stone burst from within.
Defeated, trunk shattered
Reduced slivers of slate were flung
Lost in furrow and ditch.
     YES! I shouted.

The key was turned
Engine shuddered from sleep.
As we migrated back
To motorway rivers
I marvelled at my new hands
Of the blood and the blisters.

London Bridges

The day was so clear, we could not look at each other.
Chilled air sharpened with frost
Cut on faces.
Our cheeks gorged with warm blood
Healing wounds that had not yet been made.
Walking towards the winter sun
Insulating tears held on eye lip
Swelling the light, spreading its sheerness.
We looked away but only to glass steeples
Reflecting a bleached shine back and burning coldly.
The breeze along the river's edge
Ran like a needling whisper from afar.
A threat of change reaching up from the estuary,
Reconnaissance sampling the treasures to plunder
With licks of opaline ice.

We closed ranks, ran arms together like padlocks
And continued forward. Our words
Frightened of winters bite, cosseted in our mouths.
Our stride uniformly wandering
We slid closer to river's edge.
Bare stones and chaff lay glazing in the cold.
The tide numbed and silent.
Ribs of the banks exposed in inertia,
Wanton of friction and its alms of heat.
Look at that.
My words thawing the vacuum momentarily
I raised a finger, fattened with another's leather
To the arches under the bridge.
Their grey backs in shadow, gulls
Hovered, crooked wings stretching
White bellies soaking river-top sunlight.
On a quiet wind they balanced between shelters
As a bough through seasons.
Two, side by side but not touching
Not calling to each other
The effort of navigating to stillness
Occupying them complete.

Sidings

Stuck now, locked in junctions, held between stations
It creaked to a halt, gravity like a bow wave
Still riding down the carriage.
Out of the window, browned with wind struck muck
Between the safety messages and advertisements
A shallow track.
Its bones long since taken up
Transplanted down the line.
But the sleepers too rotten to move, lay.
Oil bruised teeth tapering to a bend
Smiling at their insolence and survival.
Rust pocked where the rivets pulled
And stained so deeply they go untouched
By weeds and fronds.
Verdant hairs sprung over the track
As a spider's raw web
Fluid tipped and loose,
Unable to snag in the breeze
The spores cannot complete their march.
Drowsy boughs above, sloop
Scrawny woodlands growing over themselves.
Parched on soil islands
Cannot find the sustenance
To fill the gap where the train once was.
The hollowed space
Still shaped to the last past carriage
Un-filling though a cavity
Kept open for another breath
That does not come.

Inside my sealed cabin, endless motion;
Mouths and fingers
Legs that fidget and lives whirring
The swarmed noise of ink dipped bees.

Outside, fixed with rains, gust frozen
The frigid stillness of inutile prospering.
A flake of histories skin
Adrift and unburied.

Faery Tree

In the field by an uncle's house
Marking the centre of three acres
There was rising up
A lone tree.
Twisting stagnantly on the hillside
A lock of giant's auburn hair, wooded
Grown coarse from dormancy.

Scabbed trunk wound slowly
Corkscrewing up from sticking soil
Rarefying a four-hundred-year-old belfry
Of blossom and thorn.
That rung at Beltane day-break
Forsaken chimes
From ash tipped leaves.
Blowing unsounded
Over fallow land.

A balustrade of exposed roots
Lifted the tree from the water line.
Sipping just on errant rain drops,
Sinew weathered vines appeared below
Immersed with hollows and chambers.
Creating gateways of shade
For the creatures of the hill.

Once, among holiday ambles
The child fell towards it, lured anew
As if only now seeing it truly.
Lying back against the stump
Watching the silent actions of the farm
Peeking on labours and routines -

Familiar voices were taken
Locked away by the wind.
Looking up, a summer in bloom
Bright green clouds, sharp edged
Swayed between the light.
Long thin thorns, bobbing on the bough
As though pricking sky sea
Waiting for ripples.

Deeply set in adoring ferns
The child sank
Whilst emerald mosses grew over.
Occasional chorus of gusts
Sieved peacefully through branches
Stroked soft ears with low rush.
Trunk creaked, as arcane hinges opened
And eye lids fell.

Fitful dreams
Were pierced with new grass blades
Consciousness lanced within corporeal slumber
Leaching streams of essence
From gorging riverbed surrounds
That swept through thoughts
Hollowed and refilled
Minds-eye purged painted anew
Riven with golden spores
Washed in spectral colours
Of hidden latent hues
Lenses unfurled
Stretching between succulent muck
And temple cloud
Taken from within
Seen from outside
Sitting astride and between
Returned into

A knighted skull
Thick with power
Elongated and wide
Fattened with heft
Velveteen skin shed
Weight of newly carved antlers
Shook aloft
Sharpened in the air
Then wrapped on bulking spine
Tawny hide
Gross with vitality
Scorched grasses and flattened leaf
Falling free from wired pelt
Swelling with the curdle
Of molten blood
Pumping within
Racing veins
Lit on arteries
Enriched on each fresh lung
Raptured furnace
Fury cascading to bone
Muscles shivering with strength
Staggered hoof bundles forward
Then the other
Hallowed ground pocked in round trenches
As hoof after hoof stirs
Trips and walks
Catches stride
Then to run
Nimble and glancing
Swiftly balanced
Between haystack and hillock
Turning at the fences
Bounding from the gates
Around gently
But getting faster

Lone stampede grows
Lashed from the inside
Until antlers tooth catches briar
Shins stream blood
An under grunt
The sprint
Untethered clashing
Fences wrought
Gate smashed
Walls driven towards
Clipped then trampled
Rooftop felled
And all the while
Soil ploughed deeper
Ripped by raging hoof
Heaved beside itself
In exhausted clods
Dredged up and stamped down
Hooves trouncing arable seed
Releasing ditches
Trapped flood
Bog juices enriched
Spreading and sinking
Dipping antler
Digging troughs
Of gorse and reed
The bones of druids
Unearthed, quickly
Pummelled to powder
Carried across the field
Spread amongst the clay.

But then coldness, unexpected
Listing over freckled cheek,
Alerting fine hairs.
Arms and legs straightened
And yawning eyes opened to
Grey clouds clotted above.
Rising clumsily from the mossy bed
The child stared back
Uncle waving, calling them back.

Sitting on a concrete step
Half-awake in the late afternoon
Chewing ham and sweet bread
The child
Watched an amber train
Threading unseen town lands
And looked back at the field
Then asked the Uncle
Weren't you ever tempted to cut it down?
Wouldn't that be easier?
Not looking at the tree
He exhaled pale blue smoke, answering
Maybe... I have a saw for you
There in that shed if you wanted to do it?
The child looked back
The train almost gone
Head shaking.

Falling On

"Fall on..."
Head pulled to duty
Lowered to the
Corpulent road, harrowed in
Burden split tar.
Poxed with
Pick-shorn stones of
Beaten edges -
Shards of feast and famine
Strewn all over -
Adrift on loose camber
Awash in grit and
Grey soil.
Harvested for lifelessness.

Repellent to water
Smothering to light
Unforgiving to bone,
The incline begins to tense
On the harness.

Iron shod dead toes
Splay in the grooves.
Thumping down onto worn
Pattern of rock begetting rock.
Hammering out stowaway dew and fleck
Crushing petal and seed.

Behind which tumble the wheels,
So long torn from leaf
Moulded unnaturally from seeking the light
To the relentless roll.
Bound in black oils and woven with pins
Awaiting pull of pain splinters an
Ever axis of shine and shadow.

On heaving knees pulls
The weight of the new dead, a
Breathless tide heading for
Lands enveloped peace.
Drawn on elements seared wood
But cased in sweetened varnish
Cleaved timbers shorn up anew
By tangled iron.

Thick leather lines run neatly down the
Brass hemmed flanks
With two thin stripes astride the spine,
A ripple of slain skin
Once more flickering instruction into live nerves.

At the brow of the hill
Thickened flesh palms
Lean on blue rusted gates
And the timeworn irons open
With a familiar wail.
Weight lifted
A large amber eye, unblinkered
Casts over clouds
Breaking
Fresh dark soil and
Distant lakes, before
Returning.

Rag & Bone Man

Bring out your rags...
Bring out the cloth you split your food on
From the dinner you could not taste
The wine you cannot remember.
I'll have the half hankies torn from tea cloths
Torn from vests, flung from flesh.
Bring out furled sheets
Wrinkled in passions poverty.
The pillowcase lung
Discoloured with your thoughts.
Let's see the curtains that shielded you
As bygone dark woods.
Carpets painted with excess
Of overfull vessels
Flattened under your weight.
Roll out the towels
That wick bathed dreams from your mind
And scour reality back into your muscles.
Fling out your doormat
Caked in neighbour's mud
Trampled in by friends, hawkers
Givers and takers -
Who stood on that drawbridge awaiting
Your temperance.
Throw me the cloth you moved on from
Discarded like feigned regrets.
Worn through where harnesses cut furrows
Tie knots flowered rust
And lasso belts crushed organs.
Show me the stitches that cannot hold you any more
Broken by your growth.
The good suit that's only freedom came

In the bellies of moths.
The winter coat so sagged in rain
It formed round you like a cotton shed skin.
The straw hat you have forgotten.
Trousers bust around a green knee.
Shower me with dresses,
Past occasions locked from returning,
Though the collar holds the scent
Of futures that never came
And journeys that were missed.
Dangle me the scarf
Worn like rosary beads in the fog.
The gloves that keep
Gravestone rain from your fingers.
Then bring me your
Bones.
The aches of your ages
Haunting every morning.
Rickets in joints of youth matured
Snares of calcification.
Damage of cheques paid
Worn joints of fissions exhausted.
Hobble out the splinters of your marrow
From when you fell chasing.
The shrapnel that works the nerve
Loosened the day the loan was signed.
Bring out the ashes of your dead
Scented in polish.
Pour in there all your loss
Until the ceramic dances.
Bring it all out
I will take it all.
Refuse my eye
But fill my cart,
Brim-full with possessions.
I will hang and flail

Scrub with black water
And pan the dust.
I shall rout the sin
Entangle the joy.
I will squeeze free workday fears
Weekend laughter's.
Search for badness in the goods
Feel the sad heat on tainted gold
Knead chopping boards perished with care.
I will hear the radio stations
Of your voices in the dark.
I will dwell in the fabric memories
Slobber and sponge
Of the occurring everything
In that house.
The house, up the path
The path you will not have me tread on
Behind the door I may not enter,
Keeping the treasures
You suffocate in every day.
... Until the pony stamps her hoof
Sparking steel on cobblestone.
Lighting grime with furious flecks;
Because then, then
I know it is time
To return again
For more.

Children of Lugh

What they didn't see
When the babe was born
Was the ghost born beside it.
Between midwife and starched sheets
The spectre stretched
Recalling its limbs,
Sinews flexing to fingers
Delicately clawing the dawn air.

The child was dried and wrapped.
A cleansed white bundle
Swaddled in boiled cotton.
These adopted fibres
Plucked and weaved elsewhere
Imported over oceans -
Prickled on the phantoms vapoured flesh.

A purity of ivory light
Blazed on the infant's succulent form.
Rolls of virgin muscles shone
And clouded blue eyes
Glistened in fresh oils, used anew.
The taibhse had never seen itself
Like this before.
Not in the shallow blaze of a lamp
Hearth heat tumbling.
Nor feeling blessed sunlight
Billowing over cradle.
The drawn breast however
Was warmly known.
Suckling just from sight
The spirit watched on; pale lips

Clamping nurtures kiss as
A second unbiblical chord was strung.
Lipids began to swell the belly
From the kingdom of the Mother.
The taste though
First ever, was not as expected.
The apparition could not find
Ancestral salts.

In the house the nearly silhouette, walked upstairs
Drenched in fear and unknowing.
A room – just for the bairn.
A chamber of whitewashed timbers.
Rainbow rays, trapped and slavered on walls.
Strange beasts clung in paint.
A glowing egg, fallen from
Some electric nest;
The promise of piercing shine
Forever repelling the darkness.
Not here,
A lone candle
Signalling to starlight
Through nightly black flood.
Nor gleaming ember
Clinging in a heap
Holding back the shiver
Of disconnected shadows.

When it could stray,
After prayers were given
The child curled in slumber
And it knew death would not come
That night,
The echo took its chance to wander.
It did not feel the smooth of tarmac cooling.
No footfall sounded on cobbles

As it heard from others
Observing their hide stiffened feet
Unbalance on neat rocks.
What place was this?
Where castles knitted together
Huts doubled on top,
Fountains of water
Hid in the walls,
Pockets of gas drew constant service
And braziers perched on pillars?
Dwellings shrouded so tightly
The wind could not touch you.

Sitting on a low wall
A narrow partition of dominion
As he had come to understand,
The ghost called to a ginger cat
Caught in a battlement torch
Like snow flecked fire.
Where are our kin?
The cat nestled around its feet
Then sprang to the wall beside.
Where do you roam?
I cannot go much further. Tell me,
Where is the grass?
Where is the blood in the land?
The springs of moss?
Where are the roots growing,
Creatures grazing?
How does this keep you?
The alley cat looked up
But did not answer.
Its tail swinging from the wall edge
Though a pendulum in contemplation.

As more days were revealed
The visitor recognised less.
Though pleasant, the sounds
Came from foreign instruments
Swilled in ether unmoving.
Hours were laced in servitude
Lost in toil for abandoned benefactors.
And the people
It knew not one.
They had never helped to harry or sow.
It could not always follow their tongue.
It did not see the faces of lovers and friends
And in their eyes
It could see no ghosts
Or their robes trailing behind them.

Eventually, the child took its feet.
Stepping and running
Muscle came from fat
Words from gargles
And pure blonde hair from its crown
Grew like the sun's length.
Until one day a suitcase was packed
And the apparition travelled further
Than ever before.
On metal dogs running through midnight
Angular whales, tamed and recipient.
Finally, an orange caterpillar
Racing West
Its fatness keen to bloom.

Arriving with the daybreak
The child slept deeply
Still swaying with the motion of the journey.
It was carried over the threshold
Of the white cottage.

Rousing later, distorted from the adventure
An old smell soaked the air
Bricks of ancient clays burning.
The spirit had been resting since it arrived.
Drawing down the blue grey plumes
Allowing the aerated tannins
To wash and taint its soul
In thin yellow reverberations
Of musical notes
That had once been heard.

The gossoon awoke and ran to the first room
A tide or arms and kisses welcomed
This first return.
The taibhse's cotton suit fell
And it reached down, gathering wool from the floor.

When the water came
In the cracked ceramic cup
It ran though a spring was trapped
In the cup itself,
Slaking an outstretched thirst.

When the food came from garden furrow
The child helped smear the mud
From the skins
And in swallowing found ores
From which it was starving unknown.

Running around the cottage
The child's legs carried it faster
On every saturated lung of hillside air
Until the boundary of the dwelling
Was not enough
And so sprinted to the fields.

Under the emerald crest
Of a lone tree
Breathing deeply
The child sat carefully beside the ghost.
I know you.
Yes answered the ghost
And we know this place.
Yes answered the ghost.
Yes said the child.

Printed in Great Britain
by Amazon